RUDOLF BULTMANN

MAKERS OF CONTEMPORARY THEOLOGY

EDITORS:

The Rev. Professor D. E. NINEHAM
The Rev. E. H. ROBERTSON

PAUL TILLICH, *by J. Heywood Thomas*
RUDOLF BULTMANN, *by Ian Henderson*

RUDOLF BULTMANN

by

IAN HENDERSON

LONDON
THE CAREY KINGSGATE PRESS LIMITED

The Carey Kingsgate Press Limited
6, Southampton Row,
London, W.C.1

Printed in England by
Fletcher & Son Ltd, Norwich

Contents

Preface

THIS series has been planned with the layman in view. I have therefore tried not to use technical theological terms without explaining them. Perhaps one exception is 'existential' and here the reader who comes on the word for the first time might be guided if he remembers that existential thinking is the kind of thinking which we carry on when we carry out a big decision in life such as making up our mind to marry someone or to begin life in a new country. A Christian existentialism is one which finds in Christian faith something analogous to this kind of decision. For the sake of the lay reader I have kept the number of footnotes to a minimum.

For the more theological reader I might perhaps share some of the principles which have guided me in the selection of material for the book. It seems to me that in, for example, *Jesus and the Word* and *Jesus Christ and Mythology* Bultmann sets forth some of his views with great clarity in books which are available to the English reader at low cost. I have therefore tended to concentrate on material written by Bultmann and others not hitherto available to the English reader but indispensable if one is to gain something like a balanced understanding of the problems which Bultmann has wrestled with so strenuously.

About demythologising, very much more has been written than about any other theme of Bultmann's. Having written on this subject some years ago I have tried in this book to set it in its proper perspective of Bultmann's thought as a whole.

I have read with profit and enjoyment what other men have written about Bultmann. It is invidious to mention names but I would like particularly to express my appreciation to Drs. Hartlich and Sachs (whose work has been for too long unavailable to the English reader), and of Professor Gogarten and Dr. Körner.

To Professor Bultmann himself my debt is obvious. He has

done much to make theology an exciting study in this post-war era. I have indicated points where I think his position can be criticised, but his erudition in the varied fields of New Testament scholarship, history, ontology, classical and modern literature makes him a trap for the unwary critic whose reading has been less wide. In writing of Bultmann it is all too easy to neglect the golden rule, first understand, then criticise. I only hope I have kept it.

IAN HENDERSON

The University,
Glasgow.
May, 1965.

I

Life

THE story of Rudolf Karl Bultmann can be simply told.[1] He was born in Wiefelstedt in 1884. Not only was he a son of the manse; of his male grandparents one had been a parish minister, the other a missionary. His secondary education was received at the gymnasium or grammar school of Oldenburg. His slightly older schoolfellow, the philosopher Karl Jaspers, remembers him on the playground at Oldenburg as a boy who attracted him but with whom he did not venture to become acquainted.[2] This somewhat tantalising glimpse of the boyhood of two distinguished Europeans may or may not have to do with the fact that whereas Jaspers did not seriously give himself to academic work until he gave up his law studies and became a medical student, Bultmann was already as a schoolboy at Oldenburg laying the foundations for his quite phenomenal learning. His favourite studies, he tells us, were religious instruction, German literature and Greek. He was an avid theatre and concert-goer and he enjoyed the Oldenburg years.

Of his student years which began in 1903, he says less in the one brief autobiographical sketch he has given, but he tells us the professors who influenced him most. They were Müller at Tübingen, Gunkel and Harnack at Berlin, Jülicher, Weiss and Herrmann at Marburg. His own career as a university teacher began when in 1912 he was appointed to a New Testament lectureship at Marburg. In 1916 he was called to Breslau as assistant professor and there he remained for four years. Then, after a brief spell at Giessen, he returned to Marburg in 1921, as full

[1] The main source material for this chapter is Bultmann's own essay, *Autobiographical Reflections* in *Existence and Faith*, (Collins).

[2] Karl Jaspers, Rudolf Bultmann, *Die Frage der Entmythologisierung*, (Piper, Munich), p. 113.

professor. For thirty years until his retirement in 1951 he was to hold his chair in Marburg, and there he now lives in retirement.

From what has been said above it is easy to get the impression of Bultmann as a Christian intellectual. Up to a point this impression is both true and helpful to the non-theologian who is trying to understand the storms which Bultmann's theology has sometimes let loose. The intellectual capital of Christianity – though Englishmen will not like to admit this – is in Germany. Its ecclesiastical power may be based elsewhere, in Rome and to a lesser extent in Canterbury. But in the theological faculties of Germany Christianity is thought and rethought afresh in every generation. Here the mental battle for Christianity is fought and sometimes lost, but always fought without regard for the views of any archbishop. To this world of uninhibited academic freedom Bultmann belongs and in it he has played an outstanding part. It is only natural if those who have gained their impression of Christianity in an environment more sheltered by ecclesiastical pronouncement should find his thoughts at times upsetting.

Yet that is by no means the whole story. The influences which have played a part in Bultmann's life and thought have not been exclusively theological. Of these others something must be said, though Bultmann's own reticence, modesty and ability to concentrate on the theological subject-matter make brevity incumbent here. First there is the influence of his family. It is impossible to know Professor Bultmann even slightly without realising that his wife and children have meant a great deal to him. He is a man to whom personal relations have given much and it is significant that when he applies the language of personal relations to God he considers that he is speaking analogically not mythologically.

On the other side, there is the influence of world events. Obviously a man who loses one brother in the armies of the First World War and another in the concentration camps of the Nazis has not gone unscathed by the violence and the tragedy of the first half of the century.

Bultmann's own reactions to the Nazis are interesting and revealing. Himself, as he says, no politician – a statement not without a bearing on his theology – he yet became involved in reaction against their measures at a quite early stage. On the 4 September, 1933 the General Synod of the church already dominated by a German Christian majority friendly to the Nazis met, and, besides setting up ten new bishoprics, laid down that persons of non-Aryan descent could not be ministers, and that ministers who married non-Aryans were to be deposed from the ministry. Amid the general disquiet which this aroused and which found expression in informal gatherings of ministers and laymen, the theological faculty of Marburg was asked whether it was in accordance with the gospel to exclude Jews from the ministry. It is significant that the Marburg faculty finding was that the non-Aryan decision of the General Synod was 'incompatible with the nature of the church as determined solely by the authority of holy scripture and the gospel'.[3] It was at this time too that twenty-one New Testament specialists (among them Professors Bultmann, Jeremias and Lohmeyer) issued a manifesto in which they declared that according to the witness of the New Testament, Jewish and Gentile Christians were equally fitted for office in the church. Explicit criticism of Nazism can also be found in Bultmann's essays (cf., e.g. *The Task of Theology in the Present Situation*, 1933, and *The Meaning of the Christian Faith in Creation*, 1936).[4]

Professor Bultmann would be the last to draw attention to his rejection of Nazism. We who are English-speaking Christians might be equally wise not to ignore it. The theological and exegetical views of Bultmann have sometimes been very drastically criticised in Anglo-Saxon countries as elsewhere. This is of course perfectly legitimate, but when the critic goes on to say that Bultmann is not a Christian then it is only fair that he should answer the question whether he himself has risked so much for Christianity as Bultmann has.

[3] Wilhelm Niemöllar, *Kampf und Zeugnis der Bekennenden Kirche*, (Ludwig Bechauf Verlag, Bielefeld), p. 70.
[4] Published in *Existence and Faith*.

One last point falls to be made as a corrective against an exclusively intellectualistic estimate of Bultmann. This is to draw attention to his preaching. Consistent with his theology Bultmann has taken preaching seriously. His sermons always interesting, always simple and sometimes moving should be studied by anyone who wishes a balanced picture of the man.[5]

[5] Collected and translated into English under the title: *This World and The Beyond: Marburg Sermons*, (Lutterworth).

2

Thought and Significance

Background to Bultmann 1

IN a real sense the background to Bultmann is the rise of modern biblical scholarship. Essentially this is the application of the method of historical science to the documents of the Old and New Testament. Right at the start it can be seen the application of these methods could not fail to produce problems for Christianity. These problems are latent behind the thought of Bultmann and so perhaps it is just as well to bring one or two of them into the open at once. First there is the obvious point that critical history as a scientific study did not get under way until the late eighteenth and early nineteenth century. If we make use of its methods to determine our interpretation of scripture, can we expect that our version of Christianity will coincide with that of those who lived before the rise of critical history, e.g. the compilers of the Westminster Confession, The Thirty-Nine Articles, and, *a fortiori*, of the Nicene Creed?

Secondly, how does interpretation of scripture by the methods of historical science relate to the kind of interpretation a text gets from a preacher at a Sunday service? Most sermons are only too obviously not historical studies. The question is whether that is a criticism of them or whether they are meant to be something quite different. Here we are on one of the main issues of Bultmann's theology.

Thirdly, if study of the Bible is to take place by the methods of historical science, then are Old Testament and New Testament specialists simply historians whose particular source happens to be the documents of the Bible?

These are problems of hermeneutics which is the study of the principles of interpretation. They are quite formidable problems which no thinking Christian can escape. All Bultmann's work has a bearing on them and, if I may say so, you do not solve them just by calling him Teutonic, or a heretic.

Having said this, we have made it clear that any sketch of the background to Bultmann's thoughts must be highly selective if it is to be included in a book of this size. Fortunately the work has been done in German by Hartlich and Sachs in a book which Bultmann himself has commended.[6] What I have done in the remainder of this chapter is to avail myself of their research, particularly on Eichhorn and Gabler. It contains material inaccessible to the English reader and it has the merit of showing how the word 'myth' was introduced into biblical exposition, not by the enemies of Christianity but by its defenders.

The word 'myth' is used in several different senses by writers from Plato to Professor Cassirer. In order to grasp how it is used by Bultmann, it is not unimportant to understand how and in what sense it first came to be used in biblical interpretation, the study to which Professor Bultmann has primarily devoted his life. Among the first to introduce it into that field of study were Eichhorn (1752–1827) and Gabler (1753–1826). They did so with a positive aim – to defend the Bible from the ridicule of its enemies and in particular from those who contended that the biblical writers were just plain liars.

Unlike their opponents, the Deists, Eichhorn and Gabler were historically minded and they attempted to see the documents of the Old Testament as conditioned by their time. It is important to note, however, that they rejected the theory of Accommodation which had been expounded by Semler. Semler had contended that a good deal in the New Testament was what it was because Christ had accommodated himself to the (often primitive and undeveloped) ideas of his time. Eichhorn and Gabler tended to stick to the Old Testament and to avoid saying much about Christ. But on general principles they rejected the theory of Accommodation.

[6] The source for this chapter is the invaluable work by Christian Hartlich and Walter Sachs, *Der Ursprung des Mythosbegriffes in der modernen. Bibelwissenschaft,* (J. C. B. Mohr, Tübingen).

You are, they considered, entitled to hold that the author of a biblical book is accommodating himself to the views of his contemporaries which he does not himself share, if you have evidence for that in the text, but not on dogmatic (e.g. Christological) grounds. This illustrates a still wider principle which Eichhorn and Gabler made fundamental; dogmatics has to depend on exegesis and not vice versa.

Eichhorn and Gabler asked the biblical (and in particular, the Old Testament) exegete to come to his task not with dogmatic presuppositions, but with historical imagination. Let him stop trying to interpret his text with our present-day philosophical conceptions of God's nature and effects. To do this is to betray the Bible rather than to expound it. Instead the exegete should remember that the language of the early biblical documents is the language of the childhood of the race. That is what Eichhorn and Gabler meant by saying that these documents are written in the language of myth.

Among the features of this primitive form of language are the following: an inability to get away from what is directly present to the senses, an ignorance of causes and consequently an attributing of all events to God. The latter holds of psychical as well as physical events, and consequently the changing thoughts of a man's mind are put down as a dialogue between himself and God. Thus Cain has hardly killed Abel when naturally enough the thought occurs to him that people will ask where his brother is. There is no visible cause for this thought, therefore he ascribes it to God, i.e. God is speaking to him. Similarly the thoughts aroused in a man by the action of an animal are ascribed by man to the speech of the animal. Another feature of mythical language is the inability to form abstract nouns. Their place is taken by verbs. A story, that is to say, takes the place of a concept. To take a non-biblical example, being unable to reach the conception of self-love, the primitive mind instead tells the myth of Narcissus.

In applying their views Eichhorn and Gabler considered that they were calling for consistency. They called for consistency between biblical and non-biblical interpretations. The same

canons should be applied to biblical literature as to secular literature of the same period. That meant that if, for instance, you
didn't believe in nectar and ambrosia then you had no right to
believe in a tree of knowledge. They also called for consistency
within the interpretation of the Bible; for example, you must not
understand Genesis 2 allegorically if you understand Genesis 3
literally or, to take another example, you cannot have a real Eve
and a figurative serpent.

Other and negative principles of hermeneutics developed by
Eichhorn and Gabler include the following:

1. They rejected the allegorical method of interpretation of
   scripture unless they had evidence that the author intended
   to write an allegory. Allegory they took as the expression
   of a high mode of culture where the author had a wide
   choice of means of expression and deliberately took a fanci-
   ful one. Myth, on the other hand, reflects poverty of expression. This criticism of the allegorical method drove
   Eichhorn into attack on Kant who in his *Religion within the
   Limits of Mere Reason* had seemed to advocate it.
2. They rejected the view that the Pentateuch was dictated to
   Moses by God. They considered that this interpretation
   was ruled out by the discovery of the elohistic and jahwistic
   sources of Genesis, by the similarity to other myths and by
   the recognition that the Pentateuch was an oriental book.

Eichhorn and Gabler took over a classification of myths into
three different kinds, historical, poetical and philosophical, and
therefore they also took over the task of distinguishing between
the three. In the first there is a historical kern, though this is described in the language of myth (e.g. the fall of Jericho). But
because of the lack of abstract concepts (see above) a philosophical myth is sometimes handed down in historical terms (e.g.
the tower of Babel). Hence it is sometimes hard to distinguish
between the two. Nonetheless it can remain vital to do so, as we
can see if we consider the resurrection stories in the gospels.
According to Eichhorn and Gabler these contain myth and the

all important question is, what kind of myth – philosophical or historical?

This implies the extension of the category of myth to the New Testament. The obvious question is, if, as the exponents of this school of interpretation maintain, myth is the language of the childhood of the race, what right have we to apply it to the interpretation of the New Testament which dates from a relatively advanced period in civilisation? The reasons given for the extension of the category of myth to the New Testament are the following:

1. If you consider certain conceptions in the Old Testament are mythical, then you cannot help doing the same when they reappear in the New Testament.
2. Putting God as direct cause and personification and interpretation of a train of thought as a dialogue (see above), all of which were taken to be examples of mythical thinking, occur in the New Testament also.
3. The general principle of the economy of the miraculous remains. That is to say, everything that can be explained on natural terms must be explained.

This is obviously the most questionable of the principles of Eichhorn and Gabler, for it seems to indicate a quite *a priori* rejection of the miraculous without examining the evidence for it. Perhaps two things should be said in this connection. One is that both Eichhorn and Gabler had a radical distrust of orientals as eyewitnesses. They considered that the latter could never see facts as it were naked but only as mixed up with what they considered to be their interpretation. The other is – and here we anticipate a little – Bultmann's interpretation of miracles rests on quite different grounds from those of Eichhorn and Gabler.

Most of their readers will share Bultmann's appreciation of Hartlich and Sachs. They have portrayed in its small beginnings the stream at which Bultmann stands at the flood. They have shown with great clarity the hermeneutical canons which have

followed from the application of historical methods to the study
of the Bible. We may sum up their findings as follows:

1. The same canons of interpretation are to be applied to
   sacred as to secular texts. For example, if you reject nectar
   and ambrosia you have no right to accept manna.
2. Considerations from dogmatic theology must not be
   allowed to determine biblical interpretation but rather vice
   versa.

These are the two main hermeneutical principles laid down at
the beginning of modern biblical study. Almost equally important in present day continental theology are two other features
of the historical approach, also noted by Hartlich and Sachs.

1. The historian's professional reluctance to ascribe a historical event to divine causality. To take the non-biblical
   example of the voices which Joan of Arc heard and which
   moved her to such momentous actions. The historian will
   note that the English had a vested interest in denying their
   divine origin and the French a vested interest in main-
   taining it. And there perhaps he will be content to leave the
   matter.
2. By drawing attention to the difference between historical
   and philosophical myth, Hartlich and Sachs have pointed to
   the problems which centre round the resurrection. It is
   clear that the resurrection is central in any presentation of
   Christianity. It is almost equally clear that there are legendary elements in the accounts we have of it in the four gospels; cf. the difficulty we have in reconciling the Jerusalem
   and the Galilee appearances, and the obviously difficult
   account in Matthew of conversations between the Pharisees,
   Pilate and the soldiers, which on the face of it read more like
   counter-propaganda than reportage. What historical kernel,
   if any, lies behind the sometimes legendary accounts of the
   resurrection?

These four points all come up in the work of Bultmann and it is perhaps wise to be clear at the start that the procedures which he follows, and the questions which he asks are not arbitrary but have been made inevitable by the work of his predecessors.

In the interval between Eichhorn and Bultmann, however, the historical approach to the Bible was not allowed to go unchallenged. In the next section we shall examine the nature of the challenge.

Background to Bultmann 11

Does the historian really have the key to Christianity? Before Bultmann began his work this question was asked by Martin Kähler[7] in 1896. Kähler was criticising the lives of Jesus which had been written in the nineteenth century by writers who professed by strictly historical methods to produce a biography of Jesus. It is, however, never wise to judge a movement merely by its critics and before we deal with Kähler's criticism of the historical approach to Jesus let us see why this approach is commended by a very balanced nineteenth-century theologian, A. B. Bruce.[8]

Bruce holds that the right approach to Christianity is to come to Jesus and to see *him as he is in himself*, i.e. apart from his relation to Old Testament prophecy or to whatever statements of doctrine the church chooses to make about him. That this approach to him was inculcated by Jesus himself, follows, Bruce contends, from the words to the rich young ruler. 'Why callest thou me good?' implies that we are not to call him good until we know him and we know what goodness is.

Apart from this getting to know Jesus as he is in himself, the affirmation of the divinity of Christ is pointless. 'It is of no avail, I must repeat, to call an unknown man, still less a misconceived man, God.' Further on the same page is the sentence, 'All we really know of God in spirit and in very truth we know through

[7] M. Kähler, *Der sogenannte historische Jesus und der geschichtliche biblische Christus*, (Chr. Kaiser Verlag, Munich).
[8] A. B. Bruce's *Apologetics*, (T. & T. Clark), gives among other things an example of a nineteenth century historical approach to Jesus.

Jesus; but only on condition that we truly know Jesus himself as revealed to us in the pages of evangelical history.'

But is there history in the evangelical records? Are not even the first three evangelists more concerned with the religious interpretation of the facts than with the facts themselves? The importance of this question is emphasised by Bruce on pp. 351 and 352 of his *Apologetics*. Is the historical Jesus fact or fiction? If fact, you have the right to condemn other human life for not conforming to that image. If not, you have no such right. To use the language of Heidegger it is vital to know whether what is presented to us as Jesus is in fact an authentic repeatable human possibility. Further, Bruce argues that you cannot make Christianity independent of history, e.g. by constructing a picture of Christ from your meeting him in the experience of conversion. It might be argued that in such an experience Christ is disclosed as abhorring sin, as compassionate to sinners and as able and willing to save, and that these qualities can be shown to tally with what we know of Jesus from the historical picture. But Bruce argues that in his experience the person converted accepts that Jesus is like this because he is already assured of the historical picture of him.

When it comes to answering the question whether there is a genuine historical element in the first three gospels, Bruce admits that in them fact and faith are blended. Yet his conclusion is stated on p. 343 of the *Apologetics* as follows, 'To open-minded men neither unduly dogmatic nor unduly sceptical, a sufficient knowledge of the historical Jesus will not seem unattainable.' That such knowledge is possible is shown by the number of lives of Jesus which have been attempted. And even the gospels themselves (apart from the lives of Jesus) produce the impression 'this must be like the original'. It is as with a Rembrandt portrait. When we look at the expression and the detail on the painting of Rembrandt's subject, we say, 'there must have been someone like him'. So with the Jesus we read of in the gospels.

Kähler, whose immensely influential essay, *Der sogenannte historische Jesus und der geschichtliche biblische Christus*, is now being translated into English, is much more than a forerunner to Bultmann. But for our purpose we may single out those elements in this essay which have a bearing on our central study.

Kähler is not happy about the historians' approach to the New Testament. We have seen that men took a historical approach to the New Testament partly because it enabled them to by-pass the dogmatic approach of the fourth and fifth century creeds. But Kähler thinks that the historian has done less justice to the New Testament than the dogmatician. Let us examine his grounds for reaching this conclusion.

Against the historical approach, Kähler points out that as historical sources *for the life of Jesus* the gospels are inadequate. They tell us mainly about the end of his life. They say almost nothing about the external factors which moulded its development and nothing at all about the internal factors. People who write the lives of Jesus fill up the gaps in their sources with fantasy. Of course the fantasy is not pure fantasy. They base their imaginations on their experience of life as lived by themselves and other men. But for Christianity – and this is the thing Kähler returns to again and again – the point about Jesus is that he was different from other men and therefore other men's experience is not a clue to his. His divinity, or at least his non-mere-humanity, is the one thing that is attested by the whole New Testament.

Kähler's justification for calling the historical approach to Jesus a 'so-called' one is his claim that paradoxically it does not do justice to him as a historical figure. What a man is historically is what he achieves, the impression he leaves on posterity. There is not much doubt what Jesus achieved. He achieved faith in his followers. He left behind the impression that here was the victor over guilt, sin, temptation and death. But it was not the pre-resurrection Christ but the post-resurrection one that did this, 'The real Christ', says Kähler, 'is the preached Christ.'

In this famous sentence Kähler took the *kerygma* or preaching and put it in the central place in New Testament studies from which no deviation to historical method could dislodge it. The distinctive character as well as some of the stresses of

Bultmann's theology come in large measure from the intensity
with which he has striven to do justice both to the *kerygma* and
the historical method. To say this is not necessarily to accept
Kähler's view on the difference between the real Christ and the
historical Jesus. His position here might not have satisfied
Kierkegaard with his emphasis on being contemporary with
Christ any more than it did Ritschl with his pertinent question as
to whether then the real St. Francis is the St. Francis of critical
history or the St. Francis of legend.

But our purpose is not so much to criticise Kähler as to show
him laying down the questions that Bultmann later found himself constrained to take up. We can see Kähler pointing the way
toward form criticism in another point which he makes about the
historical method. The Bible documents, he agrees, can be considered as sources. But they are sources for the founding of the
primitive church. The church was founded by preaching and our
New Testament documents are sources for the sermons and
instruction of the leading men who founded it. They are not
sources which guarantee the content of their preaching. Nor are
they sources for a life of Jesus. For the latter we do not possess
sources in the strict sense but at best recollections. And these
recollections always bear the character of confessions in that they
always presuppose something and aim at something which lies on
the other side of mere historical factuality and which we call
revelation or salvation. It is clear enough that Kähler is not only
pointing forward to form criticism here. He is perhaps also query-
ing the position of Eichhorn and Gabler that New Testament
study can provide a non-dogmatic basis for Christian theology.
This is not how Kähler would put it himself, for, as we shall see,
he contends that the New Testament confessions, while going
beyond mere historical factuality, are not in themselves dogmatic.

But first let us examine another point which Kähler makes
about the New Testament documents treated as historical
sources. Of course they can be so treated. All writings can be.
Kähler cites Plato's dialogues, Dante's *Divine Comedy* and
Rousseau's novels as works which can all be treated as historical

sources for the period in which they were written. To take an example which Kähler does not take, it has been pointed out that though Jane Austen's novels are set in the period of the Napoleonic Wars, they contain no reference to that war. To that extent they are valuable historical sources as showing that the Napoleonic War had far less of an effect on the civil population than say the Second World War. No novel set in England during the period 1939 to 1945 could omit some reference to the war.

But while that is so, it is equally clear that Miss Austen no more than Plato, Dante or Rousseau wrote in order to provide a historical source for her own time. To judge their works by that criterion would be to do scant justice to them. Now is the same not true of the books of the New Testament? The aim for which the gospels were written was not to provide historical sources for the life of Jesus. Hence to see them merely as historical documents is hardly to do justice to them. They can be rightly interpreted only when we recognise that the aim of their writers was that the gospels should arouse faith in Jesus Christ through proclamation of his activity as Saviour.

Here again Kähler is probing at one of the nerve centres of hermeneutics. Is the meaning of a text always what the author means it to mean? Clearly an examiner correcting an examination paper would be quite wrong if he did not look for the meaning of the answer in what the candidate means it to mean. One doubts however if a preacher preparing a sermon on some words of a Pauline epistle is always primarily concerned to get at what St. Paul meant it to mean.

But it is time to see where Kähler moves from a negative assessment of the historical approach to the Bible to a positive assessment of the dogmatic one. The point occurs where Kähler urges that if Jesus has been at all times Lord of the church then acceptance of him cannot be just through the methods of scientific history, a study which has only just arisen. But, Kähler goes on, it might be said that the same argument can be brought against dogmatics. After all, there were Christians before Nicaea and Chalcedon. Even so Kähler thinks that the historians are in worse case than the dogmaticians. For the former, by the very nature of the subject, can never do justice to the non-merely-human character of Jesus. For them the divinity of Christ, like his resurrection, can at best be a problem. Dogmatics, on the other hand, with all its powers is simply at this point the attempt to defend the catechetical sentence 'true God and true man'. This Kähler thinks can be held fast to without dogmatics. Basically it is simply the assertion that Jesus can be the object of faith without that faith conflicting with the first commandment. Perhaps it is just this about Jesus Christ which contemporary theology would consider to be attested in the *kerygma*. If so, then what Kähler has done has been to leave behind a conception of the *kerygma* which can be dealt with adequately neither by history nor dogmatics (though more by the latter than by the former).

But it is time now to see how Bultmann has dealt with some of the problems bequeathed to him by his predecessors.

Form Criticism

Form criticism, the study with which Bultmann's name was associated particularly in the earlier years of his professorship, can be seen as an attempt to take seriously Kähler's criticisms of the historical approach to the Bible. The form critics came from the background of such an approach. Karl Ludwig Schmidt, one of them, says[9] that their own roots go back to literary criticism and the life of Jesus school. But, he adds, they were all convinced that this movement had got into a cul-de-sac and that the criticisms of Kähler must be taken seriously.

What this meant was that the form critics began to examine the biblical text in order to find out how far and for what it could rank as historical source material. Under Gunkel form criticism began with a study of Old Testament material. Under Dibelius, K. L. Schmidt and Bultmann it turned to an examination of the contents of the synoptic gospels, with a view to ascertaining what

[9] In an essay in the symposium, *Jesus Christus im Zeugnis der Heiligen schrift und der Kirche*, (Chr. Kaiser Verlag, Munich).

degree of reliance can be placed in them as historical source material. As such, form criticism became a highly technical branch of New Testament scholarship and readers who would like a detailed treatment of its method and results would be well advised to turn to a book like Bultmann's own *History of the Synoptic Tradition*.[10] All that can be done in a work like the present is to show how form criticism is related to the main questions which have shaped Professor Bultmann's theological thinking as a whole.

If form criticism is study of the gospels as historical sources, what are they historical sources for? Here form criticism follows up a hint given by Kähler. Primarily the gospels give us a glimpse into the period after Jesus' death when the primitive church was defining its standpoints, settling controversies and coming to some sort of terms with its environment. It is in the light of this situation that the gospel stories can best be understood. But only the isolated anecdotes and sayings go back to this point. The linkings which bind them and the locations and times which place and date them are not source material at all. They are simply literary devices conventional in character, 'on a ship', 'on a journey', 'in a house where he was a guest', which a later editor has had recourse to in order to turn his mass of material into a unity. As K. L. Schmidt says, we do not have the story of Jesus, we only have stories about Jesus.

But do we have even that? If the individual passages are primarily sources for a period after Jesus' death can they tell us anything about his life? The answer of the form critics is that if you classify the individual passages into such groups as miracle stories, controversial sayings, apophthegmata (scenes which form the framework of an utterance), prophecies and the like, each of these groups have certain fixed forms. Whether or not the forms are intact provides a valuable clue as to whether the passage belongs to a primary or secondary tradition, that is, whether as it stands, it is an earlier or a later source.

Bultmann, for instance, studies the forms of miracle stories and

[10] R. Bultmann, *History of the Synoptic Tradition*, (Blackwell).

finds such recurring factors as a description of the nature and extent of the illness, contact by hand on the part of the healer, the astonishment of the onlookers. All these are genuine features of an original miracle story. Where there is what Bultmann calls novelistic material, e.g. a tendency to name and give a rôle to minor characters, then the material is secondary. Or to take another category, what Bultmann calls apophthegmata are minor scenes depicted to provide framework for an important utterance. Bultmann tells us that you can date apophthegmata by looking at the connection between scene and saying. If the connection is so close that you cannot understand the one without the other, then the specimen is an old one. If the connection between scene and saying is loose, then the material is later.

Thus, to take an inelegant metaphor, the form critic determines the age of gospel stories and sayings by looking at their forms in somewhat the same way as a horse dealer tells the age of horses by looking at their teeth.

Now, other things being equal, the older an account is, i.e. the more nearly contemporary it is to the event which it describes, the better it is as an historical source. Form criticism therefore, whatever else it is, is an attempt to examine the synoptic gospels as historical source material. The result of the examination is to find that *judged from this standpoint*, the synoptics are like the curate's egg, good in parts. There is no attempt on the part of Bultmann to say that Christianity stands or falls by this examination. On the contrary, Christianity then as now stands by the *kerygma* or preaching which is found in such passages as Romans 1: 3, 6: 3, 10: 9; 1 Corinthians 11: 23–26, 15: 3–7; Philippians 2: 6–11 as well as Acts 2: 22–24, 3: 13–15, 10: 37–41 and 13: 26–31. The synoptic passages were only handed down to implement the *kerygma*. Their function is ancillary.

This, I think, is how Bultmann would use his form criticism work. There is a real sense in which he and Barth agree with Kähler, or at any rate, at one point, did agree with him, namely that behind the *kerygma* you cannot go. You must either accept it or reject it and that is that.

Christianity does not then stand or fall by the examination of the synoptics as historical sources. To say that does not commit one to an approval of the results of the examination as carried out by Bultmann. It may be that he had found too many parts of the egg bad and too few good. This is an obvious place where Bultmann may well be open to criticism of those who are competent New Testament scholars. But it would be a pity if that criticism were to blind us to the burden which was laid on the shoulders of men like Bultmann and K. L. Schmidt and Dibelius by Kähler. They may have made mistakes in carrying out the task. But the task of evaluating source material for the words and deeds of Jesus had to be carried out.

Principalities and Powers

For Collingwood, the English historian and philosopher, Bultmann has no little respect. Quite independently and working in different fields, the two men reached not dissimilar viewpoints. It is therefore perhaps appropriate if we use Collingwood's description of the historians' task to throw light on one of the difficulties of applying the methods of modern history to the documents of the Bible.

In his *Idea of History* Collingwood makes the point that the method of the historian is different from that of the natural scientist. When the latter asks 'why did this piece of litmus paper turn pink?' he is asking on what kinds of occasion does blue litmus paper turn pink. But when the historian says 'why did Brutus stab Caesar?' he is asking what did Brutus think that made him stab Caesar.[11]

Thus for Collingwood, success as a historian depends on one's ability to think the thoughts of a man like Brutus. The ultimate causal factors in history are thoughts. Further, though Collingwood is not concerned to make this point, the assumption is that these ultimate causal factors are human thoughts. The historian

[11] Collingwood, *Idea of History*, (Oxford), p. 214.

may through his knowledge of the human possibilities and situations be in a position to think the thoughts of Brutus. He is hardly in a position to think the thoughts of God. For all his differences from the natural scientist, the historian, if he speaks simply as a historian, must when God is suggested to him as a causal factor reply in the words of Laplace to Napoleon, 'I have no need of that hypothesis!'

So that one difficulty of applying historical method to the documents of the Bible is that a good number of the actions in the Bible are ascribed to non-human causes. This kind of causation may exist. Sometimes, indeed, those who take part in history, like the Air Marshal at the time of the Battle of Britain, are convinced that it exists. But it is not something with which history *qua* history can deal.

If biblical criticism is simply the attempt to apply the canons of critical history to the documents of scripture, what is it to make of this apparent checkmate? Let us begin by asking how modern theology deals with this problem when actions in the Bible are ascribed neither to God nor to man. Here we come up against the principalities and powers of the Authorised Version. The Greek words thus translated are ἀρχαὶ and ἐξουσίαι or δυνάμεις in Romans 8: 38; Ephesians 6: 12; Colossians 2: 15; but in Galatians 4: 9 and Colossians 2: 8 and 20 the same beings are called the στοιχεῖα τοῦ κόσμου, the elements of the universe to whom St. Paul thinks his Galatian converts are in danger of again coming in bondage if they adopt a Jewish legalism into their Christianity.

It is clear then that some of the people to whom St. Paul wrote believed in the existence of these demonic beings, possessing a certain cosmic status and having dominion over the lives of at least some men and women. That they were thought to possess causal efficacy is clear from one passage where the Cross itself is ascribed to their agency. None of the ἀρχόντες possessed a knowledge of the wisdom of God, says St. Paul in 1 Corinthians 2: 6, otherwise they would not have crucified the Lord of Glory. For the historian the execution of Jesus is essentially a Roman judicial act, no doubt a miscarriage of justice. What is he to make of this ascription of it to supra-human demonic beings?

It is the different answers which different theologians give to this question which shed light on some of the theological alternatives of our generation. Bultmann's solution to the problem, interesting as it is in itself, can only be appreciated if we see it over against some of the alternatives.

Thus it is perhaps not generally realised that the highly courageous attitude toward the war which Professor Karl Barth took up in the years 1940 and 1941 was based on a quite literal acceptance of the powers and principalities. The prospects of allied victory during these years were not exactly bright but Barth never despaired of it.[12] Resident almost within sight of German territory and marked out for dispatch to a concentration camp should the German army add his own small country to the list of those it had already invaded, Barth did not for a moment despair. Instead he adjured the French Protestants not to accept final defeat as the will of God, and in 1941 sent his letter of encouragement to the Christians in Great Britain. In the latter he adjured his British friends not to base their resistance to Hitler on natural law (a conception which his translator felt it necessary to explain to them in a footnote). Natural law, Barth claimed, led to the twilight where all cats are grey. It led – to Munich. Christians in Britain as elsewhere ought to base their resistance to Hitler on Jesus Christ. For are we not told in Colossians 2: 15 of Christ's victory over the ἐξουσίαι? 'Having spoiled principalities and powers he made a show of them openly, triumphing over them in it?' What has this to do with Hitler? Barth finds the link in the fact that in Romans 13 the state is referred to as one of the ἐξουσίαι. Hitler's demonic state is one of the ἐξουσίαι triumphed over by Christ. We who are Christians therefore would do well not to take it too seriously and not to doubt of its final overthrow.

[12] For Barth's position with regard to the 1939–45 war see his essay *Rechtfertigung und Recht* and the various documents translated and edited by Professor R. Gregor Smith under the title *Against the Stream*, (S.C.M.).

It goes without saying that in 1941 this was a brave and real faith. It is a faith which interprets world history in terms of the New Testament. But it is a New Testament to which the historian does not have the key. For the historian cannot take demonic agency at its face value any more than the psychiatrist can.

In the writings of yet another twentieth-century theologian, Professor Burkitt, the principalities and powers get different treatment.[13] Unlike Bultmann, Burkitt does not consider Gnosticism as a rival religion to Christianity. He thinks of the Gnostics rather as Christians who tried to reconcile their religion with the advanced science of their day. That science was represented notably by the Ptolemaic astronomy and astrology. We know now that this has been outmoded by Galileo and Copernicus. But in its own day it marked an important advance. It was based on scientific observation of the heavens and was an attempt to 'save the appearances'. As a result of this the view was put forward that the earth was surrounded by a transparent rotating sphere on which the stars were fixed. Then it seemed reasonable to give the same explanation for the five planets then known and for the moon and the sun whose motions bear no relation to the fixed stars. Hence each of these is thought of as being a sphere on its own which also revolved round the earth. Thus the earth was thought of as surrounded by transparent but rigid spheres in much the same way as the heart of an onion is surrounded by its outer layers. This view stressed the importance of the planets, each of which was thought to be Lord of a sphere which surrounded the earth and therefore exercised an influence over it and over those who lived on it. Hence the basis, not wholly unscientific, of astrology, and of the demonic beings, the powers and principalities of the New Testament. At the time of the appearance of Christianity, Burkitt argues, this was the view of the advanced scientific man and it made him look askance at the Old Testament whose cosmology is much simpler, heaven being

[13] Burkitt's views are expounded in his book *Church and Gnosis*, unfortunately out of print.

supported on pillars raised from the flat floor of the earth. Thus in Isaiah 40: 22 and Psalm 104: 2, the firmament or vault of heaven is described in terms of a cover, curtain or roof for the earth. In II Samuel 22: 8; Job 26: 11; Proverbs 8: 27–29 this cover is thought of as resting on pillars or mountains of the earth. So that Burkitt's point is that to offer the Old Testament (which was of course the Bible of the early church) to educated citizens of the Roman empire was like offering a literal acceptance of the book of Genesis to members of the British Association today. The Gnostics were, in fact, the modernists of their day who reinterpreted Christianity in terms of contemporary science. They were in fact the first exponents of apologetical thinking.

For Burkitt then the principalities and powers are concepts of an out-of-date science. They are science discards, rather like phlogiston. When the historian meets a reference to phlogiston in an eighteenth-century document, he knows what is meant by this substance which was considered to be a part of all combustible bodies. But he also knows that science has long since ceased to hold this view of combustion. Hence the historian when he comes on an account of something as caused by phlogiston, simply rejects the account. Similarly, on Burkitt's view, one can only reject any account of the principalities and powers as operative factors in the universe.

The interesting thing about Bultmann's position is that he offers a third alternative to Barth and Burkitt. Instead of simply accepting the principalities and powers as Barth does, or simply rejecting them as Burkitt does, he interprets them. He would claim that his interpretation is biblical in that it is simply following St. Paul's own interpretation of the principalities and powers. Further he claims that St. Paul's interpretation is existential, i.e. an interpretation in terms of human will and decision. That is to say, in terms of the causal factors which the historian can understand. It is clear that if Bultmann's contentions are correct the central problem of biblical scholarship, how far the New Testament is open to the methods of the historian, is in some way nearer solution. It is time, therefore, to study Bultmann's treatment of the principalities and powers in some detail. To do so we have to consider his view of Gnosticism. Like Burkitt, he holds that the principalities and powers are Gnostic concepts. Unlike Burkitt he holds that Gnosticism is not a Christian and perhaps heretical attitude to contemporary science, but rather a non-Christian religion. His view of Gnosticism is based on his acceptance of the Mandaean writings as providing a clue to its nature.[14]

For a long time the Gnostics were known to Christian thought chiefly through the writings of their opponents, especially Irenaeus. This is never the most satisfactory source of information and it is not surprising that modern scholars have made a good deal of relatively recent discoveries which have given them a more direct knowledge of what the Gnostics actually taught. Among these are the sacred books of the Mandaean religion, one of them called The Ginza or The Treasure, the other The Book of John or The Book of the Kings.

The Mandaean cult involves baptism, and repeated baptism at that. The teaching of their books is very much akin to what we from other sources would call Gnostic. One half of The Ginza, for instance, is called the book of the dead. The thesis is that when a Mandaean dies, there is confusion among the rulers of the material world. They gather together and say, 'who has taken away the pearl that illumined the falling house? In the house that it has left the walls cracked and fell in'. Here we have a piece of what Bultmann outlines as the basic Gnostic myth. Pneumatic souls are a part of the heavenly being who has been imprisoned by the demons in the world. For the soul to escape means that its prison collapses. So the demons who have created the world (out of the captive heavenly being) naturally try to intercept the escaping soul and prevent its departure. But the power of the baptisms which the soul has undergone in life enables it to elude the demonic powers and to escape to the realms of light to which it really belongs. The soul then has a long and difficult journey

[14] For an account of the Mandaean writings see V. Burch, *The Structure and Message of Saint John's Gospel*, (Hopkinson).

after death; the frontier guards try to stop it on its way to its true home in the realms of light. But because of its ability to speak the name of the chief of the realms of light, which has been imparted to the Mandaeans by the latter heavenly personage and which has been spoken over the latter in baptism, the soul has, as it were, the password and is able to reach its true home.

Are the Mandaeans Christian? Against this would seem to be the fact that in the books they are warned against Eshu Mshiha (Jesus Messiah) as a deceiver. He is said to be one of the demonic beings and will in the future be unmasked as such. The true Lord is said to be Anush-Uthra who came into the world in the days of Pilatus, carried out miracles, imparted the true teaching and then departed to the realms of light.

There are pretty close parallels between passages in The Ginza and passages in the fourth gospel. Bultmann, who is concerned to find in the Mandaean writings a clue to a non-Christian source of some of the fourth gospel, quotes some of these in his commentary on St. John, 'Fear not and be not afraid and say not, they have left me alone in this world of evil. For I will soon come to you.' 'Whenever you seek me, you will find me; whenever you call, I will answer. I am not far from you.' Other Mandaean writings give us, 'Thou showest us the way on which thou hast come from the house of life.' Bultmann maintains that the eschatology of John 14 is not the traditional eschatology of Jew and Christian, the resurrection of the dead and the last judgment. It is rather concerned with the fate of the individual soul, which after death, through the guidance of its redeemer, escapes to its true home. It is for this reason that he sees in the Mandaean writings evidence of the Gnostic teaching which infiltrated into the New Testament.

Bultmann offers an account of what might be called basic Gnosticism.[15] It is a cosmology, a myth to the effect that demonic powers have succeeded in capturing a being from the realms of light. This is the original cosmic fall and since then this heavenly

[15] For Bultmann's treatment of the basic Gnostic myth see his *Theologie des Neuen Testaments*, pp. 164 ff.

c

being of whom spiritual 'pneumatic' individuals are parts, has been kept prisoner by the demons in a structure which is, in fact, the world as we know it. Redemption comes when another heavenly being, this time the image of the most high, comes down from the realms of light. Here on earth the Redeemer appears disguised in earthly form so as to avoid recognition by the demons. He imparts gnosis, knowledge, to the pneumatic individuals and finally leaves again for the realms of light, having instructed his followers how they may come after him in safety. He has thus outwitted the demonic powers and broken up their world. There is coupled with this the belief that the Redeemer and the pneumatic soul constitute one body and hence whatever happens to him, happens to them.

So much for the Gnostic myth. The first thing one wants to know is whether there is evidence of it independently of and chronologically prior to the New Testament writings. There is evidence of its existence in the Mandaean writings, but whether these are chronologically prior to the New Testament writings is a question on which experts differ, Professor Stauffer and F. C. Burkitt, for instance, holding the opposite view to that of Professor Bultmann.

That being so, the next thing the non-specialist wants to know is, does the Gnostic myth enable him to understand otherwise obscure passages in the New Testament? I think it certainly does. Passages in John 14, whose beauty often leads us to forget their difficulty, do become meaningful in the light of this myth. So does the verse, 1 Corinthians 2: 8, which runs 'had the princes of this world known, they would never have crucified the Lord of Glory'. That sentence obviously springs from a different world of thought from our own, and Bultmann's reconstruction of the Gnostic myth does give us some insight into that world.

But if Bultmann sheds light, he also arouses embarrassment. For are we to say that all the views which have been founded on this element in the New Testament, say, the kenotic christology, Kierkegaard's doctrine of the divine incognito, or in a different connection, the view that the church is the body of Christ, are not really Christian but Gnostic? Not all that is founded on an illusion is illusory, but it is surely disquieting to find that views which have nourished the piety of Christians, and which were originally sincerely put forward as expositions of Christianity, are not really so.

On this point Bultmann has several things to say. For one thing, he does not lack admiration for Gnosticism. He considers that it shares with Christianity the distinction of seeing for the first time the utter difference of human existence from all worldly existence. That, from one who stands so near Heidegger as Bultmann does, is praise indeed. Further Bultmann considers that Gnosticism did Christianity a real service in presenting it with a *Begrifflichkeit*, a word which Mr. Grobel translates 'terminology'. Then he recognises, of course, that the New Testament maintains, in opposition to Gnosticism, that the world is the creation of God and not of the demonic powers who in Romans 8 are themselves described as created things. Finally, Bultmann holds that St. Paul copes with Gnosticism by interpreting its cosmology existentially.

What does that mean? Well, Bultmann's thesis is that St. Paul introduced a new factor, the human will, into the situation depicted by the Gnostics. Bultmann's exposition of the Pauline anthropology – for him the very heart of Christianity – consists in showing how this new factor reacts on the Gnostic entities of the demonic powers, the cosmos and the tomblike body in which the spirit of man is imprisoned and how they in turn react on it. Let us consider, for example, the world. Unlike the Gnostics, who think of it as brought into being by demonic powers, St. Paul considers it the creation of God. As such it only becomes the rival of God, and so demonic, when man, as we are told in Romans 1, chooses to worship it rather than the creator. Thus, as Bultmann says, it is ultimately from man himself that the demonic beings derive their power.

On this view, the pathos of the human situation lies in the fact that having been given their power by the decision of man, the demonic forces of the world then proceed to tyrannise over that same human will. The way in which this takes places comes out in St. Paul's treatment of the other Gnostic idea of σῶμα σῆμα, the body a tomb. Bultmann does not have much difficulty in showing that for St. Paul the σῶμα means not only the body but also the self in so far as it is an object to itself (or the subject of the actions of others). The tragedy of the human situation is that this self is at variance with the self to which it is an object (what St. Paul calls the inward man or the mind). When an individual chooses to worship the creature rather than the creator and so build his life on what is under his control, whether it be material things or his own achievements, he finds paradoxically that he loses control over his own self and that it rises up in mutiny against him in the kind of situation described in Romans 7. If you want a modern illustration, think of some rich person who builds his life on the material things he has at his disposal and then in the end finds himself in a psychiatrist's consulting room because what St. Paul would call his σῶμα is doing strange things that he does not like and cannot control. In such a situation the principalities and powers have gained their entrance into the citadel of man's self, and his σῶμα, at variance with his inward man, has become a tomb. But again this happened ultimately because of man's own decision.

Deliverance comes when a man decides for Christ; that is, when he decides to find his security not in material things nor in his own achievements, but in the salvation which God gives him in Christ. Then the entire picture changes. The demonic figures lose their power. For the Christian they no longer exist save as the possibility of a fall from faith. The world is no longer a rival to the creator, the self is harmonised with itself and the σῶμα no longer a tomb. Further, on this existentialist view, the true gnosis is seen not as a quasi-natural knowledge but as man's appreciation of the new possibility of his existence which is given to him by God in Christ, a possibility for which he may decide whenever the gospel is preached to him.

Demythologising

This is perhaps the best place to say a little on a theme about which much has already been written, the demythologising controversy. For full treatment of it the reader must be referred to *Kerygma and Myth* and to some of the many books which have been written on it.[16] All that need be said here is that in 1941 Bultmann published an essay *Neues Testament und Mythologie* in which he drew a distinction between two things in the New Testament. On the one hand there is the Christian gospel as true today as ever and on the other the first century world view, mythological in character, which modern man cannot possibly accept and which is not specifically Christian anyway. The treatment of the latter element which Bultmann recommended was *Entmythologisierung*, demythologising. By demythologising Bultmann did not mean eliminating the mythology but interpreting it existentially, i.e. in terms of man's understanding of his own existence and possibilities.

In the main the controversy has been carried out in Germany with fairness and charity. But inevitably what has been written in the controversy has tended to highlight and to isolate certain aspects of Bultmann's thought at the expense of others. The present chapter is meant simply as a mild corrective to this process.

Bultmann's position in the demythologising controversy was one which his New Testament studies committed him to. It is impossible to read his *Theology of the New Testament* without realising that for him St. Paul's teaching on the σῶμα (translated as the objective aspect of the self, rather than as the body) comes very near to disclosing the heart of the Christian gospel. In that teaching, as we found in the last chapter, Bultmann sees St. Paul not as rejecting but as interpreting existentially the mythology of

[16] The English translation of the original documents of the controversy is published under the title *Kerygma and Myth*, (Harper & Brothers, New York). Professor Bultmann's own *Jesus Christ and Mythology*, (S.C.M.), should also be read. Of the books written in English about the controversy Professor John Macquarrie's *An Existentialist Theology*, (S.C.M.), gives a very full and clear treatment of the philosophical issues behind the controversy. My own views are published in *Myth in the New Testament*, (S.C.M.).

Gnosticism. But this kind of interpretation of a myth in terms of human possibilities and decisions is just what is meant by demythologising.

Hence if we interpret the New Testament existentially we are simply continuing a process begun by the earliest and one of the greatest of New Testament writers. Further, by stating it in terms of a presentation of human possibilities and decisions we are doing two widely different but equally essential things to the New Testament. First we are giving the ordinary man of today not a demonology nor a discarded science but a gospel concerning which he must decide for or against. For we are forcing him to decide whether the possibilities for human existence which its myths express are possibilities that he can accept for his own existence. And there here again we are keeping close to the original presentation of Christianity in the form of *kerygma*. Thus when St. Paul preached on Mars Hill he did not merely give a Gifford Lecture. He preached and we are told the decisions that men made about his preaching. Some mocked, some deferred and some believed.

Secondly and on a quite different level, by translating the myths of the New Testament into human possibilities and decisions we are making the New Testament amenable to the historian whose method, as we have seen, can only deal with humanly initiated actions.

Here we come on what is perhaps the real centre of Bultmann's thought, certainly the element which gives it its most distinctive quality, the fact that as regards the New Testament he is both historian and evangelist. It is not easy for any man to fill both these rôles. We cannot say how successfully Bultmann does so until we have examined his interpretation of the statement 'God acts', a statement essential to the evangelist and intractable to the historian. For the present let us content ourselves with noting that existential interpretation of scripture, or as it has come to be known, demythologising, is what gives Bultmann his chance to fill both these two rôles of historian and evangelist, neither of which he finds himself able to renounce.

We have seen that the controversy about myth drew disproportionate attention to one of the many essays which Bultmann has written and which are collected in the three volumes of *Glauben und Verstehen*. It was this one essay, *New Testament and Mythology*, which brought Bultmann, hitherto known as a New Testament critic of great distinction, into the centre of the field of systematic theology. Further, this essay changed the theme of systematic theology. Apologetics in the sense of discourse with the non-Christian, valiantly maintained by Heim but discredited by Barth and even Brunner suddenly became theologically respectable again. More than twenty years after its publication we can perhaps now raise the question why this one essay of Bultmann's raised the storm it did.

The date, 1941, is significant. During the years of the Nazi régime the church in Germany passed through a severe crisis. Hitler's creed of racialism was incompatible with a religion which holds that in Christ there is neither Greek nor Jew. For tactical reasons Hitler could when it suited him gloss over this incompatibility and in this he was aided by the so-called German Christians. For them Jesus was an Aryan hero. Their favourite gospel was the fourth, with its derogatory references to the Jews and the voice of Hitler was God's call to the Germans of the day. The following extract from a sermon by Bishop Coch gives an idea of what their preaching was like: 'A good shepherd has been given to our people, Adolf Hitler. All the qualities which the Bible ascribes to the good shepherd are united in his person. A new faith is kindled by his Christianity of action . . . '.[17] The Confessional Church formed to withstand this danger had in Bultmann a loyal and consistent member. But few will deny that the theologian who influenced it most in its beginnings was Karl Barth. His rejection of natural theology, so unintelligible across the English Channel, was in fact a summons to the church to break with those who claimed that God spoke to them in Adolf Hitler. This conviction of his is embodied in the famous

[17] Quoted in W. Niemöller, *Kampf und Zevgnis der Bekennenden Kirche*, (Ludwig Bechauf Verlag, Bielefeld), p. 137.

'Barthian' clause of the Declaration of the Synod of Barmen in 1934. It runs as follows, 'Jesus Christ as he is attested to us in holy scripture is the one word of God, which we have to hear, to put our trust in both in life and in death, and to obey'.

Few of those who were Barth's students in the years before the war will deny that he had a word for the time. For the church faced with heresy within and persecution without, the time was one for witness. It was understandable that Christians so hard pressed should tend to clinch an argument with the words 'es steht geschrieben' ('it is written'), and follow them with a text from scripture. It was not a time for biblical criticism and the hard-pressed confessional was ready to find in Barth support for the view that he who tried to go behind the witness of the apostles was abandoning himself to purely subjective criteria of what Jesus Christ must be. It was easy and indeed natural to gain the impression that the issues of historical criticism had been settled and need no longer concern the young theologian who had so much else to worry about.

War and allied victory broke up this situation. War brought the inevitable mingling of Christian and non-Christian. It was followed by an allied victory in which Nazism was swept away and with it the curious heresy of the German Christians. All the problems presented by historical criticism revived along with the atmosphere in which they could be discussed. The Christian found himself in a salon instead of an arena. Bultmann's essay on myth, whatever else it did, helped him to make the adjustment between the two places. It would be a great mistake unduly to stress the contrast between Barth and Bultmann. But it is relatively easy to understand why the one has dominated the pre-war and the other the post-war theological situation.

Two questions remain for discussion in this very brief chapter on the controversy about myth. They concern its extent and its outcome.

There are different ways of gauging the lengths to which Bultmann goes in the controversy. It has been debated, for instance, whether Bultmann sees any limits to demythologising.[18] I do not know if this minor controversy about the controversy is very important. On the one hand, wherever Bultmann sees myths, he demythologises them and to that extent there is no limit to demythologising. On the other hand, Bultmann sees the Christ event as an act of God in the analogical not in the mythological sense and therefore in the last resort as something which does not admit of demythologising. What Bultmann means by an act of God is something we must deal with in the next chapter.

More important is perhaps to ask whether Bultmann's position in the controversy about myth leaves open the possibility of the kind of christology we find in the statements of Nicaea and Chalcedon. I do not think it does. On Bultmann's interpretation, what Christian faith does is to give me a new understanding of my own existence. There is nothing particularly subjective in the merely psychological sense in this view of faith. As Bultmann says, a child's self-understanding manifests itself in the love, trust, feeling of security, thankfulness, which he has toward his parents. My self-understanding can hardly change without a change coming into my relationship with other people, my work and my surroundings.

So much must be granted to Bultmann. But the question still remains, what kind of statements, if any, does faith allow me to make about the person of Christ? At the very outset it can be said that it does not allow me to make the kind of statement which is made in the traditional creeds. Bultmann ascribes this kind of thinking which went to the making of the formulae of Nicaea or Chalcedon to the Greek tradition. For it – and this holds of the thinking of the heretics as well as of the orthodox – is thinking about the φύσις, the nature of Christ. Within the New Testament itself, a knowledge of the nature of Christ unaccompanied by a knowledge of myself is to be found in the knowledge of or belief in Jesus which is possessed by the evil spirits in St. Mark's gospel or by the demons in the epistle of James. But for the rest, the pronouncements which the New Testament makes about

[18] By Dr. Schubert M. Ogden in his *Christ without Myth*, (Collins).

D

Jesus are, Bultmann claims, not about his nature but about his significance (Bedeutsamkeit), i.e. about what God says to me through him. That such are Bultmann's views would seem to follow from the important essay in which he discusses the christological confession of the Oecumenical Council.[19]

If we ask why the kind of statement about the relation between God and man in Christ that is found in the ancient creeds should not commend itself to Bultmann and those who think like him, several reasons can be suggested. On the exegetical level, Bultmann considers that the expression 'son of God', when found in primitive Christianity simply has the sense of an oriental royal title. To interpret it as implying the possession of a divine quality in the metaphysical sense, as is done admittedly as early as the epistle to the Hebrews, is to misinterpret it. Then it seems to be that Bultmann's consistently held opinion that when God and man come together they do so in meeting (Begegnung) and not in a union of two natures. To use the latter phrase of man, and still more of God would seem to imply that the categories applicable to inanimate objects can be used also to describe the living. And that is precisely what Heidegger – whose influence on Bultmann is by no means negligible – warns his readers against. It might also be argued that the very notion of a timeless human nature with which the divine could be united in itself implied that man has his true being outside the concrete, actual meetings and decisions of life. And that is something which Bultmann would certainly not accept.

Now this issue is quite vital. For all the signs are that Christianity is going to split on the christologies of Nicaea and Chalcedon. On the one hand the ecclesiastical power structures which dominate the ecumenical movement will hardly settle for anything less in the one church they are manoeuvring for. It is significant that a catholic theologian otherwise most sympathetic to Tillich accused him of 'betraying Christ' because his viewpoint was incompatible with Nicaea and Chalcedon.[20] It is per-

[19] *Glauben und Verstehen*, Band II, p. 246.
[20] G. H. Tavard, *Paul Tillich and the Christian Message*, (Burns Oates), p. 2.

haps not unfair to see in this the typical standpoint of the power theologians, if we may apply this term to those theologians whose views reflect the standpoint and provide the apologetic for ecclesiastical power concentrations. On the other hand there are those whom we may call the influence theologians, men like Bultmann and Tillich, who make no effort to dominate or reproduce the views of ecclesiastical power groups but who have perhaps a much greater influence over 'fringe Christians' or 'fringe non-Christians' than any comparable power theologians. One can hardly see much place for either Tillich or Bultmann in the one church that the ecumenical movement is exerting its immense pressures to bring about.

Concerning the outcome of the controversy about myth the reader will, after due perusal of the relevant literature, make his own assessment. On the one hand one cannot but feel sympathy for those who are put off by the negativities of Bultmann. In the face of 1 Corinthians 15, the earliest and best of the sources, is it all that easy to rule out what is called however crudely an objective Resurrection? On the other hand it would be quite unfair to refuse to recognise the positive behind the negative in Bultmann. For him the Resurrection is something here and now. It is entering into a new dimension of existence, a being set free from the past and from guilt and from care and being made open to one's fellow-men in love. When one reads one of Bultmann's great evangelical sentences like the one in the most controversial of all his essays where he describes how the believer has confidence 'That what is invisible, unknown, outside his control covers him as love . . . and means for him not death but life', one may still disagree with Bultmann for setting aside evidence for an objective Resurrection. But one must in fairness admit that *if* one had to choose, one would prefer Bultmann's account of the Resurrection to one which sees it simply as the reanimation of a corpse.

Perhaps something of a final word on the outcome of the controversy has been said, I think, by Professor Fuchs in one of his essays. Fuchs points out that we can all at least envisage a

situation where we might be persecuted for our Christian faith.
We can further envisage ourselves trying to face up to such a situation by asking ourselves what amount of suffering it will involve
us in and what help we may expect from God. There is no doubt
that we would count on receiving such help in our need. There
is equally no doubt that we would not expect it to take the form
of an angel opening our cell door after the manner of Acts 5 : 19.
We just would not reckon with such a possibility. To that extent
we have all, whatever our theological affiliations, demythologised. And so to that extent Bultmann has won the controversy
about myth.

God Acts

We have seen that the problems which form the background to
Bultmann's life work arise from the application of the methods
of modern history to the text of scripture. And we have seen that
the thoughts in which the modern historian finds his explanation
are human thoughts. Small wonder then that Bultmann should
demythologise the principalities. In doing so he claims to be
following in the steps of St. Paul. If Gogarten is right, Christianity by getting rid of the principalities and powers, itself began
the process of secularisation and so helped to set the universe free
for scientific explanation.[21]

Be that as it may, it is obvious that a much greater difficulty
remains. The principalities and powers are not the only greater
than human causal agents in the New Testament. God himself
acts in scripture. Does that mean that scripture is not amenable
to the treatment of the historian? Or are all passages which
describe God's actions to be demythologised? Or is there a limit
to the process of demythologising?

Bultmann's attitude to these questions, as to others, has both
a negative and a positive side. On the negative side is Bultmann's
treatment of miracles. A miracle has been defined as something
that makes us say 'Oh!' The biblical definition of miracle is much
rather something which makes us say, 'this is the Lord's doing

[21] Cf. F. Gogarten, *Verhängnis und Hoffnung der Neuzeit*, esp. pp. 106 ff.

and it is wondrous in our eyes!' In a hitherto untranslated essay[22] Bultmann deals pretty briskly with the view that God is the causal agent in what in the New Testament are presented as miracles.

In this essay there are three arguments for the negative side of Bultmann's position. The first is that to find God in miracles would be incompatible with the uniformity of causation. For Bultmann the universality of natural causation is not based on empirical generalisation nor is it primarily a scientific postulate. It is prescientific and ontological. It is tied up with action, which, and not theory, is man's primary reaction to the world in which he finds himself. Bultmann quotes Herrmann as saying, 'the simple decision to work includes the thought that the things with which we wish to work will follow a conformity to law which our thoughts can master'. It certainly would be difficult to act unless, as Bultmann says, we were pretty confident that God was not going to alter the laws of gravity at any given moment. Yet human action can cope with a certain amount of lawlessness. Gamblers can indulge in a good deal of activity despite the fact that horses are notorious for their erratic behaviour and, on a higher level, medicine is not an exact science.

A second argument against finding God at work in miracles in the natural world runs as follows. A miracle in the sense of an act brought about by supernatural causation which overrules or sets aside the natural order of things is always ambiguous. The question can always be raised, is it good or bad, does it come from God or the devil? Therefore it is inadequate to the conception of an act (*Tun*) of God. The unexpressed premiss is that God's acts reveal him for what he is. Indeed with him as with us, his acts make him what he is.

The third argument connects with Bultmann's basic conviction that it is sin that makes us look for miracles in nature. He begins by considering the specific case of the Jews. Why did they seek for signs (σημεῖα)? Because their approach to God was a radically sinful one. They were legalists. They sought, that is, to find

[22] In *Glauben und Verstehen*, Band I.

their security in their works (Leistungen). They understood
themselves in the light of their achievements and so they understood God in the light of his. That the former procedure is
wrong-headed means that the latter is also. When we have met
God in Christ and consequently no longer try to justify ourselves
by our achievements but find our security in God, then we look
at the world differently. It is no longer the sphere for achievements, our own or God's, but the sphere where we are called to
obey God and where we are now for the first time, because
delivered from fear, open to meet our fellow men in love. There
is, says Bultmann, (*Glauben und Verstehen* 1, 221) only one miracle,
that of revelation, the revelation of God's grace to the ungodly,
forgiveness. Having experienced it, we do not need to look for
miracles in the external world.

Thus, as so often happens in his thinking, Professor Bultmann's negative attitude toward miracles in the ordinary sense
of the word must be seen in the light of the positive element in
his theology. Briefly, his position is that God meets us in our own
concrete existence through grace. He meets us when the Cross of
Christ is proclaimed to us. 'He (Christ) is God's gift to the world.
At the Cross God's grace becomes manifest. God has made him
Lord, who was nothing for himself and who knew no desire to
vindicate himself (*gelten lassen*) and whom surrender and love
brought to the Cross.'[23] Through this gift of Christ a new possibility is given to us to decide for Christ, to accept the revelation
of God which he has brought. Further, the possibility is given
to us to understand our 'thrownness' (*Geworfenheit*)[24] not as
fate or destiny but grace. Finally the possibility is given us to
cease finding our security in material things or in our own
achievements but in God. We are given this possibility in 'the
faith that what is invisible, unknown, outside our control meets
us as love and means for us not death but life'. (*Kerygma and*

---

[23] *Glauben und Verstehen*, Band II, p. 154.
[24] *Geworfenheit* is a term of Heidegger's. It can be taken to mean the hand
we have been dealt in life and which we can do nothing about, – such factors
as our parents, our I.Q., our nationality.

Myth, 1, 30). This possibility comes to us through grace. 'Only he who has been loved can love, only he to whom trust is given can trust, only he who has experienced surrender, can surrender.' (*Ibid.* 43.)

For Bultmann the real miracle (*Wunder*) is this meeting with God in Christ with the consequent impartation of new possibilities to our existence. Everything else he dismissed under another name (*Mirakel*) and has little use for. We find God in our own existence, we do not find him in miracles in the ordinary sense of the word.

In his very first reply to those who criticised his programme of demythologising, Bultmann raised the subject of divine action in the following words. 'Perhaps we may say that behind all the objections raised against demythologising there lurks a fear that if it were carried to its logical conclusion it would make it impossible for us to speak of an act of God, or if we did it would only be the symbolical description of a subjective experience.'[25] The passage which follows these words, and the corresponding section of *Jesus Christ and Mythology*, show that Bultmann takes this most fundamental of the objections to demythologising very seriously. He seems to agree that if it did hold, it would be a valid criticism of his position. But he is at pains to show that it does not hold, that he can still speak, and speak non-mythologically, of the action of God. These passages are therefore obviously important as throwing light on the fundamental paradox and tension of Bultmann's thought, the fact that he is both an evangelist and a historian. As an evangelist, he is constrained to proclaim the action of God. As an historian he cannot accept it as a causal factor in the scheme of things.

Bultmann begins by saying that when he talks of God acting, he is speaking not in mythological but in analogical terms. The word 'analogy' is perhaps unfortunate for the first thing Bultmann does is to reject that God in action is like other causal agents. This is the kind of view which used to be expressed in small type on the back of steamship tickets where the shipping

[25] From *Kerygma and Myth*, E. T., p. 196.

company announced that it would not be responsible for loss or damage caused by a typhoon, the king's enemies, acts of God or piracy on the high seas. Bultmann is careful to state where he differs from such a viewpoint which thinks of God's action as at once breaking and linking the chain of events. God, he says, does not act between events but within them. The example which Bultmann takes to bring out his meaning is that of an accident which happened to us. We may come to look on it in faith as God's gift to us – presumably as bringing us to our senses – or as God's chastisement. Bultmann's implication is that this way of seeing God's hand at work in our life is perfectly legitimate. But it is of course quite compatible with the fact that in a police court the cause of the accident may be found to be a faulty brake or someone else's carelessness.

Bultmann's position here is superficially like one which other theologians have taken up. Thus Joseph Butler reaches something like a rational doctrine of providence by noting that the husbandman who is remiss with his spring sowing loses his whole year's harvest and the youth who sows his wild oats too lavishly may irrevocably lose both health and fortune, and from this advancing to the conclusion that God is dealing with men by means of rewards and punishment. But Bultmann would not hold that you are entitled to reach general conclusions about God's actions on the basis of what he does to other people. What he is saying is that in an existential moment of truth you may come to see God's hand in something that has happened to you personally. That is why it is hardly fair to say that Bultmann is really cheating, that what he calls analogical acts of God are really mythological ones. It is neither necessary nor possible to demythologise an analogical statement about the action of God because demythologisation is existential interpretation and analogical statements about God's action are already expressed in existential terms in an existential situation and cannot really be transposed out of that situation into general terms. In practice they often are in doctrinal theology. But Bultmann holds that this is illegitimate. One can understand him when he says that the person who really believes in the omnipresence of God is the prisoner-of-war. And one can understand Barth too when he claims that Bultmann has reduced christology to soteriology. Barth[26] quotes a sentence in which Bultmann says of the crucifixion, 'it is not the saving event (*Heilsereignis*) because it is the Cross of Christ rather is it the Cross of Christ because it is the saving event'

Has Bultmann got hold of something here? I think he has got hold of the important point that the meaning which those who take part in history find in it may not be the same as the meaning that the historian finds in it. We can perhaps illustrate this by an example from the history of our own century. Henning von Tresckow, the man who put the bomb in Hitler's aeroplane, shot himself after the final failure of the 20 July conspiracy. His last words were, 'It may be that as God once spared Sodom because there were ten righteous men in it, so he will spare Germany because of what we have done.' These words were spoken in a situation of great extremity, where evil had triumphed over good, where God seemed to have turned away his face and where for the speaker there was no way but death. These words inspire respect because they are spoken in faith in such a situation. They would not have the weight they do if they were uttered by a spectator looking at the plot from the outside. Nor would we expect to find a historian dealing with post-war Germany to find one of the causal factors for its remarkable economic recovery in God's attitude to the 20 July conspirators.

Bultmann's position here may seem to circumscribe God, to limit his action to the existential situations of the life of the individual. It might be asked if God is not also at work in the wider world without, in the course of universal history and in the centuries of recorded and unrecorded time? If Bultmann is not unduly concerned to find God at work in such a wider field, the reason is that he does not take these concepts of the world, history and time quite at their face value. He follows Heidegger in

[26] In *Rudolf Bultmann, ein Versuch, ihn zu verstehen*, (Evangelischer verlag A. G. Zollikon-Zürich), p. 21.

holding that basically they are all existentials, that is basic forms
of human existence. The world is that into which we are thrown,
willy-nilly. It is that with which we have to do and to come to
terms. History is the sphere where existents decide between the
possibilities open to them, sometimes on the basis of their assessment of the decisions of existents in the past. Time, too, is that
way of existing in which man even as he stands at the moment of
the present knows himself bound to a past and open to a future
which has an end. A world in the sense of extended matter, history in the sense of universal history and time in the sense of
clock time are rather artificial constructs formed from these basic
aspects of human existence. The theologian then will not be
unduly disconcerted if he finds God at work not in the former
but only in the latter.

For a fuller treatment of Bultmann's relation to Heidegger's
philosophy the reader must be referred elsewhere.[27] But some
account of it, however brief and fragmentary, was necessary here.
For the divine action is the point where three Bultmanns meet,
Bultmann the evangelist, Bultmann the historian and Bultmann
the philosopher. If the critic often thinks it is the point where he
can refute Bultmann, the reason may be that his approach to it is
more one-sided than that of the sage of Marburg!

Jesus and the Gospel

Jesus as a historical figure is the subject of works written by
Bultmann during the early, middle and later periods of his activity
as a New Testament specialist. To the early period belongs the
book translated into English under the title, *Jesus and the Word*,
but called in the original simply *Jesus*. To the middle period be-
long the thirty-two pages about Jesus at the beginning of the
German original of his *Theology of the New Testament*. Most re-
cently we have his Heidelberg essay (1962), *Das Verhältnis der
urchristlichen Christusbotschaft zum historischen Jesus*, written in reply

[27] E.g. to J. Macquarrie, *An Existentialist Theology*, (S.C.M.), and J. Körner,
Eschatologie und Geschichte, (Herbert Reich, Hamburg).

to younger scholars, some of them his own pupils who feel they can say more about Jesus than Bultmann can.

Bultmann, speaking as a historian who has examined critically the sources which we call the New Testament does limit himself in what he says about Jesus. Bultmann's Jesus has no consciousness of being the Messiah. He never predicted his passion nor did he imagine that he would return again to earth. He was mistaken in his belief in the imminent end of the world.

These are negative features in Bultmann's portrait of Jesus. It would be a pity if they kept us from seeing the positive features, for Bultmann's Jesus, if he is an attenuated figure, is a relevant one to the situation of our own day. He is a wandering existentialist teacher, making no concession to the nationalism of his day. He is in protest against a tradition which once bore a relation to the life of his country but which no longer makes sense. He departs from legalism and calls men instead to make a radical decision between God and his realm on the one hand and the world on the other. In a passage like Mark 3 : 4 we find him telling men that they must not make loyalty to an institution like the sabbath a pretext for shirking the decision between good and evil. For if men decide for God, they must love their neighbour. For Jesus, says Bultmann, 'there is no obedience to God which does not have to prove itself in the concrete situation of meeting one's neighbour'.

Such a portrait of Jesus may be inadequate but it is at least relevant.[28] It is easier for Germans to see this, living as they do in a country where the consequences of a nationalism run riot have been only too obvious and where traditional institutions and the moralities they impose on their members have collapsed. But to say that is not just to say that Bultmann has depicted a Jesus who meets the German need. It is perhaps rather that it is easier for the Germans to see the common European situation more clearly. Things have been less drastic in England and so much more of

[28] Most of this paragraph I wrote originally for a Third Programme review of Bultmann's *Theology of the New Testament* in 1953. But I think it can still stand.

the façade remains. English nationalism has been so much less violent and pernicious than the German variety that it is hard for Englishmen themselves to realise how immensely strong it is and how many thoughtful people elsewhere see it today as one great barrier in the way of Europe's one hope of survival-federation. The façade of so many English traditions, the tradition of the working-class movement, the public schools remain. Hence it is natural for English Christians to find Christian action in a support of the morality and the loyalties of these traditions, whether they be of the left wing or the right wing, without asking whether they do not presuppose an England that has ceased to exist. At a time when the great European sortie is over and its destinies are being decided by men who live outside its borders, it may be that the best and indeed the only form of Christian action for the European Christian is to meet one's neighbour in love in the concrete situation where one finds him. It may be that the imperative binding on the Christian today is not the moral code which membership of an élite class with Christian overtones, whether it be the Prussian officer or the English gentleman, entails, but simply to be a man who is open to his neighbour of any class or creed and able to enter into an I–Thou relation with him.

These are at any rate arguable themes and to come to grips with them is, according to Bultmann, the way to come face to face with Jesus. To try and penetrate to his personality is to miss his purpose. The thing to do, Bultmann tells us in the introduction to his *Jesus and the Word*, is to let his words meet us with the question of how we are to interpret our own existence. And Bultmann's presentation of Jesus is relevant to our own existence. The Anglican who makes considerable sacrifices to send his son to a public school founded in the Victorian era to create a ruling class for an empire that no longer exists; the Catholic who sincerely holds to a law governing marital intercourse framed in an age when a man of thirty got a wife of thirteen as part of a package deal in business or politics and when infant mortality was appalling, may well have sound theological reasons for rejecting Bultmann's portrait of Jesus. Into the intricacies of christological argument we cannot enter in a book of this nature. But even if they have not, they cannot accept Bultmann's portrait of Jesus. For they are holding fast to the very standpoint which Bultmann rightly or wrongly maintained that he opposed.

Bultmann's Jesus is thus a controversial figure and not just an attenuated one. Recent controversy in the Jesus of history debate has centred round the attempt to give him more positive content and in particular to link up more closely than Bultmann does the Jesus who is known by the historian with the Christ who is preached by the evangelist. Here again we can only touch upon a fascinating chapter in contemporary theology. Suffice to say that Professors Fuchs, Ebeling and Bornkamm[29] all consider that they can say something more about the historical Jesus and that that something more identifies him more closely than Bultmann does with the gospel preached to us. Fuchs finds the key to Jesus in his actions and particularly in his fellowship at table with outcastes. By this he testified that the very people who have most cause to flee from God are those who will find a refuge in him. And this is just the message of the gospel. Ebeling finds the key to Jesus in faith. To have an encounter with him was to be summoned to have faith. His own death was a venture of faith. Hence when the church preaches a risen Christ here and now, it is being true to the historical Jesus. Bornkamm finds the key to Jesus in the directness with which he met men and women. What he did in these rather terrifying encounters was to make the present real to them, the present in which they lived and had to decide. Here again there is a link between the historical Jesus and the gospel which is preached to us and summons us to have faith in our particular situation now and to love the particular person we find a headache at the moment.

Now Bultmann in his Heidelberg essay of 1962 has made it clear that he will not link the Jesus of the historian and the gospel

[29] The works of these three writers are now available in English under the following titles: Günther Bornkamm, *Jesus of Nazareth*, (Hodder & Stoughton), Gerhard Ebeling, *Word and Faith*, (S.C.M.), Ernst Fuchs, *Studies of the Historical Jesus*, (S.C.M.).

of the evangelist as closely as the three thinkers I have mentioned. He criticises them for not clearly distinguishing between historical investigation into the sayings and acts of Jesus and an existential encounter with Jesus. The latter presupposes the former. To those criticised this may seem a little hard, for passages are not wanting in Bultmann's works where he stresses the existential nature of historical study. But here as elsewhere one gets the impression of Bultmann refusing to relax the tensions. In this case it is perhaps the tension between the New Testament professor during the week legitimately exercising all his critical faculties in the historical study of a New Testament passage and the same professor in church on Sunday having the same passage preached to him and knowing that if he now has recourse to his critical historical faculties he will simply be evading the gospel's summons to decision.

A further position which Bultmann takes up in the Heidelberg essay is that the gospel only presupposes the 'that' and not the 'what' of Jesus. It is concerned that is to say only with the fact of Jesus' existence and not with what kind of a man he was. Here again those criticised may feel that there are passages in Bultmann's other works which contradict that standpoint. When Bultmann, for instance, in an essay describes the crucified Christ as, 'He, who was nothing for himself and knew no desire to count for something, whom surrender and love brought to the cross . . . ',[30] does his description not presuppose some knowledge of what sort of a person Jesus actually was? And when Bultmann in a fine passage says, 'It is only he who has been loved who can love; only he in whom faith has been placed, who can have faith, only he who has experienced surrender, who can surrender himself. We are set free to give ourselves to God because he has given himself for us.'[31] Many Christians might feel that their assurance here is not unconnected with what they know of the surrender and love of the historical Jesus.

But it would be wrong to close without pointing out that, here

[30] *Glauben und Verstehen*, Band II, p. 154.
[31] *Kerygma und Mythos* I, p. 43.

as elsewhere, behind the negativities of Bultmann's position, lie his positive affirmations. If Bultmann is ready to surrender what he regards as the outworks it is because he considers that the central citadel is intact. The *kerygma*, the gospel is that in Christ God meets man here and now and offers him a new possibility of understanding his own existence. That, and not a set of historical data, is for Bultmann, rightly or wrongly, the centre of Christianity. In the Heidelberg essay he writes, 'It is often said, and mostly in a critical sense, that on my interpretation of the *kerygma*, Jesus has risen into the *kerygma*. I accept this way of putting it.' If we may use aristotelian and thomistic language to describe the position of an existential theologian, what we have in Bultmann is something like a doctrine of the Real Presence in the preaching of the word.